T0001362

Hiqelem

1000 years ago...
Hiqelem
Hiqelem

This story is an interpretation
of a time and place.

This book is dedicated to the Sts'ailes people.
A big thank you to Morgan Ritchie for all his help.

Copyright © 2015 by Scot Ritchie

All rights reserved. No part of this publication may be reproduced, stored in a retrieval system or transmitted, in any form or by any means, without the prior written consent of the publisher or a license from The Canadian Copyright Licensing Agency (Access Copyright). For an Access Copyright license, visit www.accesscopyright.ca or call toll free to 1-800-893-5777.

Published in 2015 by Groundwood Books / House of Anansi Press
groundwoodbooks.com
First paperback edition 2023

We gratefully acknowledge for their financial support of our publishing program the Canada Council for the Arts, the Ontario Arts Council and the Government of Canada.

Canada Council for the Arts | Conseil des Arts du Canada

ONTARIO ARTS COUNCIL
CONSEIL DES ARTS DE L'ONTARIO
an Ontario government agency
un organisme du gouvernement de l'Ontario

With the participation of the Government of Canada
Avec la participation du gouvernement du Canada | Canada

Library and Archives Canada Cataloguing in Publication
Title: P'ésk'a and the first salmon ceremony / Scot Ritchie.
Names: Ritchie, Scot, author, illustrator.
Identifiers: Canadiana 20230486347 | ISBN 9781773067599 (softcover)
Subjects: LCSH: Salmon fishing—Juvenile literature. | CSH: First Nations—British Columbia—Social life and customs—Juvenile literature. | CSH: First Nations—Fishing—British Columbia—Juvenile literature. | LCGFT: Picture books.
Classification: LCC E99.C49 R58 2023 | DDC j971.1004/9794—dc23

The illustrations were first drawn in pencil, followed by fine line work in ink. They were then scanned into the computer and colored in Photoshop.
Printed and bound in Canada

P'ésk'a and the First Salmon Ceremony

SCOT RITCHIE

GROUNDWOOD BOOKS
HOUSE OF ANANSI PRESS
TORONTO / BERKELEY

What if you could go back in time?

P'ésk'a opens his eyes. Today is an important day for his people — the Sts'ailes. But the special tray needed for the ceremony has been left behind!

With the tray under his arm, P'ésk'a goes looking for the Siyá:m — the chief.

Every spring P'ésk'a's people celebrate the First Salmon Ceremony. It's their way of saying thank you to the river for all the salmon it brings.

Salmon is the most important food for the Sts'ailes people, but P'ésk'a and his family also rely on other animals and berries to eat. Everything the Sts'ailes need to survive is found in the forest and the river.

These men have cut down a cedar tree to make a canoe. First, the trunk is hollowed out. Then, hot rocks and boiling water are placed inside, and the trunk is steamed over the fire to change its shape.

P'ésk'a is going to make his own canoe when he is older.

The Sts'ailes use cedar trees for many things. The ceremonial tray is made from cedar wood. Mats, baskets, hats and clothes are made from cedar bark. Even P'ésk'a's shirt is made from bark!

Everything smells so good that P'ésk'a has to stop for a minute at the smokehouse to catch his breath. Smoked salmon and dried blueberries are his favorite foods, but today there's no time for a snack.

This is where the drums are made from wood and animal skins. P'ésk'a can hear them beating clearly.

"Come to our First Salmon Ceremony," they say.

Bang! Bang! The ceremony starts when the first salmon is caught and put over the fire. There is more than enough for everyone.

P'ésk'a runs to the chief and delivers the ceremonial tray, just in time.

What a feast!

It's a good thing you're fast like a bird.

The people have finished eating, and they put the salmon bones on the ceremonial tray. The chief leads the procession. With a splash, he returns the salmon bones to the river.

Everybody thanks the river for the sth'óqwi — the greatest gift.

I wish I could go back one thousand years.

More About the Sts'ailes People

The Sts'ailes live on the Harrison River today, as they have for at least the past ten thousand years. All the ancient buildings are long gone, but if you visit, you can see where P'ésk'a ran through the village to deliver his tray.

Art was important to the Sts'ailes. It reminded them who their ancestors were. It was used for decoration on drums, clothes and baskets.

The wooly dog shown in the story was only found in this area of North America and is now extinct. Fur from these dogs was woven into blankets and clothing.

Everybody was related and many families lived together in pit houses or plank houses. Plank houses were bigger.

To make a pit house, digging sticks were used to loosen the earth. Then large pieces of wood served as shovels. This was a community effort involving twenty or more people.

Nobody knows for sure, but it is believed that one thousand years ago the population of Hiqelem was about five hundred people. There were fourteen pit houses and six plank houses.

Rocks, bones and wood were used to make things like spears, arrows and paddles.

Salmon were prepared in many ways. Some were eaten fresh, some cooked over the fire, some wind-dried, some smoked over the fire, and others cooked in underground ovens.

To bring down the giant cedar trees, the Sts'ailes used an adze (a combination of an ax and a chisel) and hot rocks. A hole was carved in the trunk of a tree so a heated rock could be placed inside to singe the wood. When the wood was soft enough, it was removed using the adze. This was repeated until the tree fell down.

Glossary

The Sts'ailes language was banned at one time, but people are learning it again thanks to community elders and teachers. Here are some words you might want to learn.

Chá:lhtel (chahl-tl) – to smoke fish
P'ésk'a (peskahh) – hummingbird
Sátet (satet) – to offer something or pass it along
Sítel (seetall) – basket
Siyá:m (she-am) – chief
Sméq'eth (smekoth) – gift of leftover food for guests to take home
Sqémél (skumel) – pit house
Sqwemá:y (skwamaih) – dog
Sth'óqwi (stow-kwey) – salmon, fish
Stó:lō (stahlo) – river people
Sts'ailes (stehles) – beating heart
Tál (tel) – mother

A Letter from Chief William Charlie of the Sts'ailes People

Dear Readers,

I am pleased to see this book, which helps bring to life the ancient life of our people. The Sts'ailes are actively revitalizing our history, language and culture through education, both for our own people and for others, and this book will be a valuable tool in this ongoing effort.

Scot Ritchie's artistic expression of Sts'ailes life and culture is based on careful research and is also very respectfully executed. I am glad that it will be available for children from all places to read.

For those who want to learn more, Sts'ailes is a warm and welcoming community. Maybe some day you will visit us!

Chief William Charlie
2015

Hiqelem

1000 years ago...
Hiqelem
Hiqelem

It's the day of the First Salmon Ceremony, when P'ésk'a and his people will give thanks to the river for the salmon it brings. But when P'ésk'a wakes up, he sees that the special tray needed for the ceremony has been left behind ...

"Ritchie successfully and engagingly balances storytelling with accurate history in this depiction of Indigenous life." *Booklist*

"A good initial introduction to a lesser-known First Nations people." *Kirkus Reviews*

"The combination of lively pictures and informative text makes this a winner for primary collections in school and public libraries. Recommended."
CM Magazine

$14.99
Cover art © Scot Ritchie
Cover design by Michael Solomon
Also available as an ebook

GROUNDWOOD BOOKS
HOUSE OF ANANSI PRESS

Groundwood Books is grateful for the opportunity to share stories and make books on the Traditional Territory of many Nations, including the Anishinabeg, the Wendat and the Haudenosaunee. It is also the Treaty Lands of the Mississaugas of the Credit. In partnership with Indigenous writers, illustrators, editors and translators, we commit to publishing stories that reflect the experiences of Indigenous Peoples. For more about our work and values, visit us at groundwoodbooks.com.

ISBN: 978-1-77306-759-9